MARCELLA'S HOUSE

PLAYHOUSE

TOOL SHED

PLAYROOM

Books open the
world to your child

A PARENTS' GUIDE
TO
RAGGEDY ANN & ANDY'S
GROW-AND-LEARN LIBRARY

A LYNX BOOK

This book is published by Lynx Books, a division of Lynx Communications, Inc., 41 Madison Avenue, New York, New York 10010. The name "Lynx" together with the logotype consisting of a stylized head of a lynx is a trademark of Lynx Communications, Inc.

Raggedy Ann and Andy's Grow-and-Learn Library, the names and depictions of Raggedy Ann, Raggedy Andy and all related characters are trademarks of Macmillan, Inc.

How the
GROW-AND-LEARN LIBRARY
Can Help Your Child

Dear Parent,

According to Dr. Benjamin Spock, a child's personality is most actively developed during the early years. This development does not occur overnight. It occurs as a result of many different experiences.

Raggedy Ann and Andy's Grow-and-Learn Library was designed with just this development in mind. These books are more than a library of delightful stories for your child to enjoy; they also deal with subjects that were carefully chosen to help you establish a firm foundation for your child's growth.

Every parent and grandparent—in fact, every person who knows and loves a small child—has experienced the joy that comes from sitting with that child and reading wonderful stories. This warm, intimate time brings you closer together and gives you an opportunity to share feelings and talk about the things that matter most during the growing-up years, and throughout life.

Raggedy Ann and Andy's Grow-and-Learn Library addresses basic childhood experiences—sharing and caring, fears and hopes. Wise Raggedy Ann, along with her adventuresome brother, Raggedy Andy, and all their playroom friends spring to life when they are left alone. The dolls live and play together, meet new friends, and journey out on a series of exciting adventures. Together they face and overcome a variety of childhood problems and learn to cope with the world around them.

Young children will identify with the dolls and will understand the dilemmas they face. And reading these stories with your child provides a wonderful opportunity to explore real-life situations. How a child deals with early experiences is an important factor in how that child copes later in life. By thinking and talking about their feelings and emotions, children develop self-confidence and feel better about themselves.

With Raggedy Ann and Andy's Grow-and-Learn Library, you can help your child develop the social and emotional tools that are needed to succeed in this very complex world. This series also helps develop a love of reading and good books. William Bennett, U.S. Secretary of Education, has said that, if teachers and parents encourage children to read, then "the world will open for them." Don't miss the opportunity to open that world to your children, and also to open the road to an understanding and communication that will last a lifetime.

LOUIS WOLFE
Chairman and Chief Executive Officer
Lynx Communications, Inc.

How to Use the Parents' Guide

This parents' guide was designed to help you—and your child—get the most out of this very special library. You'll learn how each of the stories can be enhanced and extended by the use of special activities and read-with-me suggestions.

As you look through the following pages, you'll find a special section devoted to each of the 19 books in Raggedy Ann and Andy's Grow-and-Learn Library. Each section covers the following:

About the Story: Meet the featured characters and read a synopsis of the story.

About the Theme: Each story focuses on a subject that early childhood experts agree is important to your child's social and emotional growth and to his or her ability to cope with preschool problems.

Among the subjects treated are:

> *Building self-esteem*
> *Building self-confidence*
> *Learning to express feelings*
> *Overcoming shyness*
> *Overcoming jealousy*
> *Overcoming fear of separation*
> *Making friends*
> *Considering people's feelings*
> *Sharing*
> *Cooperating*
> *Respecting others' property*
> *Accepting responsibility*
> *Interacting with others*
> *Solving problems*
> *Making the best of things*

Suppose you feel your child has a problem with jealousy—perhaps in a relationship with a sibling or with a friend. Just glance through the About the Theme paragraphs, and you'll find that volume 4, *Raggedy Dog to the Rescue*, would be a perfect conversation-starter.

Reading the Story: This series of questions will help assure you that your child has understood the story. While thinking about the answer to each question, your child will focus on the story's theme and its gentle lessons. Answering the questions can also lead to a broader discussion of your child's feelings about the theme.

Reading Between the Lines: Here is further motivation for you and your child to discuss the implications of each story. Most children don't feel free to talk about their innermost feelings and fears, even if they have a great need to do so. Once your child has explored how the storybook characters felt in different situations, you can move naturally into a discussion of what he or she might have done in similar circumstances. This will encourage your child to consider how the theme of the story relates to his or her life.

Grow-and-Learn Activities: The operative word is *fun*. These activities are meant to be shared by you and your child. In some, you can be an active participant; in others, you can encourage your child to do the activity alone and show you the results.

Grow-and-Learn Library: Although each book in the library is independent, the themes and characters overlap, balancing one another. Here you will find other titles in the series that complement the book you are reading.

VOLUME 1
SUNNY BUNNY COMES HOME

About the Story

One rainy day Marcella discovers long-lost Sunny Bunny in
the attic. She brings him to the playroom and leaves
him in the company of the other dolls. They
welcome him by displaying the talents that make each
of them special. This leaves Sunny Bunny wondering if
he, too, is special in any way. An accident provides
Sunny Bunny with the opportunity to discover that he is
indeed special. He earns the respect of the
others by using his unique ability to leap high in the
air to save Marcella's balloons.

About the Theme

Sunny Bunny Comes Home illustrates the theme you are special.
Whether it is due to having red hair, wearing glasses,
being able to read, or being able to leap high in the air,
each and every person in the whole world is unique and special.
Reading and discussing this story will help your child realize
that he or she is also special.

Reading the Story

Read *Sunny Bunny Comes Home* with your child. Talk about what is happening in the pictures. Ask your child questions such as the following to assure understanding of the story.

1. Where did Marcella Find Sunny Bunny? (In the attic.)

2. To whom did Sunny Bunny belong? (Marcella's mother, when she was a little girl.)

3. How did Raggedy Andy show that he is special? (By doing cartwheels.)

4. How did Babette show that she is special? (By doing a graceful dance.)

5. How did Sunny Bunny show that he is special? (By jumping high to catch the balloons.)

Have your child turn the pages of the book and tell what is happening in each picture. Then have your child tell the whole story in his or her own words.

Reading Between the Lines

Ask your child to tell what Sunny Bunny learned in this story—that everyone in the playroom is special and that *he is special, too.* Be sure your child understands the concept of being special—being an individual who is not exactly like anyone else in the world.

Your Child and Being Special

Encourage your child to name some characteristics, talents, or traits that make him or her special. These can be quite simple, such as having freckles, being able to tie shoelaces, being nice to cats, helping others, or being an only sister. Emphasize that each person is special in a different way, but nonetheless special.

Discuss how other members of the family are special. They may be alike in some ways, but each has a unique combination of personality traits and abilities. Talk about ways in which your child's friends are special, too.

Grow-and-Learn Activities

Comparing Have your child draw three hearts on a piece of paper, color them red, and cut them out. Ask him or her to compare the hearts (it may help to lay them on top of each other). They may look very much alike at first, but one may be smaller, one longer, and one may have a wiggly edge. Point out that each one is special in its own way. You can repeat the activity with three blue squares or three green triangles.

Collecting Pictures Give your child several old magazines and ask him or her to find pictures of cars. Lay the pictures out side by side. Then help your child name things that are different about the cars (color, style, make) and things that are the same about them (four wheels, headlights, windows). Your child might enjoy cutting out the pictures and putting them in a scrapbook, sorted according to color or some other characteristic.

Self-Portrait Your child may enjoy drawing a self-portrait that shows some of the things that make him or her special (These could range from having curly hair to wearing glasses!). You can help by printing your child's name and I Am Special at the top of the paper. Display the artwork on your refrigerator or in some other prominent place.

Grow-and-Learn Library

A related story in Raggedy Ann and Andy's Grow-and-Learn Library is *What Can a Camel Do?* (Volume 5). This tale illustrates the theme everyone can do something special. For another story featuring Sunny Bunny, see Volume 16, *The Sleepover.*

LITTLE BEAR'S PROBLEM

About the Story

Raggedy Ann and Raggedy Andy visit the circus with Marcella. There they meet Little Bear, who is unhappy because his parents must perform in the circus and cannot spend much time with him. Raggedy Ann and Raggedy Andy show Little Bear what wonderful things his parents are doing when they are away from him and how these things bring much enjoyment to others. Little Bear comes to understand and accept the situation and to focus on *his* future as a circus performer.

About the Theme

Little Bear's Problem examines the feelings experienced when a child is away from home and parents. These feelings often include loneliness, confusion, and fear of rejection. Reading and discussing this story will help your child understand that even though they may have to be away from home from time to time, parents always love their children.

Reading the Story

Read *Little Bear's Problem* with your child. Allow your child to help turn the pages of the book as you discuss what is happening in each of the pictures. Ask questions such as the following to assure understanding.

1. Where did Marcella take Raggedy Ann and Raggedy Andy? (To the circus.)

2. Where did Marcella leave Raggedy Ann and Raggedy Andy while she watched the circus? (Near Little Bear's cage.)

3. Why was Little Bear sad? (Because he wanted to be with his parents.)

4. How did Raggedy Ann and Raggedy Andy help Little Bear? (By pulling back the tent flap so he could watch his parents perform.)

5. What does Little Bear want to do when he grows up? (Perform in the circus, like his parents.)

Reading Between the Lines

Ask your child to describe how Little Bear felt about being away from his parents at the beginning of the story. How did he feel when he saw his parents performing? Then ask how Little Bear felt at the end of the story. What made Little Bear change his mind? Have your child describe what he or she thinks Little Bear will do from now on when his parents are away.

Your Child and Being Away

Ask your child to tell how he or she feels both when you go away from home and when you return. Discuss what your child does while you are away.

Point out that being alone makes it possible to do many wonderful things, such as drawing, playing with toys, pretending, and learning a new game or activity. You can bring up other influencing factors, such as who stays with your child when you are gone (a favorite grandparent or babysitter) and where your child might stay. This is also a good time to explain some of the things you do when you are away—work at your job, like Little Bear's parents; do household errands or go shopping; visit with grown-up friends. Perhaps you can arrange for your child to visit your place of work.

Grow-and-Learn Activities

At Home and Away Ask your child to show you one enjoyable activity to do while you are away. Do not take part in the activity, but allow your child to describe it to you. Then ask your child to tell you one of his or her favorite things to do when you are at home, such as play a quiet game or watch television with you. Arrange to participate in that activity with your child as soon as you can.

Making a Clock A toy clock may help your child understand when you'll return home after an outing. Use a white paper plate. Help your child cut a large and a small hand out of paper. Punch a hole in the center of the plate and attach the hands with a paper fastener. Place this clock next to a real clock. Help your child write numbers in the appropriate places on the paper clock. The next time you go out, arrange the hands of the play clock to show the time you will return. Your child will learn to compare clocks and know when to expect you to return home.

Pretending Allow your child to dress in grown-up clothes and pretend to be a parent. What do you do at work? Suggest that your child act out what you do on your job (for example: typing, selling, or driving a truck). Talk about the people you work with: what they do and if they also have children. Have your child show what a parent might do when a child is away.

Grow-and-Learn Library

This story can be supplemented by Volume 16, *The Sleepover*, which explores the theme of sleeping away from home.

SAM LAMB MOVES AWAY

About the Story

When Marcella's visiting cousin David returns home, she gives him her toy, Sam Lamb, so that he will remember their time together. Since the dolls miss Sam, they devise a plan to contact him. They ask their friends the sparrows to deliver letters to Sam. When the sparrows return, the dolls learn that although Sam misses them, too, he has made many new friends. The dolls promise to write often and to remain friends with Sam Lamb even though he lives far away.

About the Theme

Sam Lamb Moves Away is a story about friendship; it tells what happens when a friend moves away. A friend's moving away does not mean that the friendship has ended. A new kind of friendship can begin. Sharing this story can help prepare your child for a time when a friend moves away.

Reading the Story

Ask your child to look at the pictures while you read the story aloud. After you have finished the story, ask questions such as the following to be sure your child understood the story.

1. Why did Marcella give Sam Lamb to David? (So he would remember their time together.)

2. Where does Sam Lamb live now? (At David's house.)

3. How did the dolls send letters to Sam? (By having sparrows deliver the letters.)

4. Was Sam happy in his new room? (Yes.)

5. How did the dolls plan to stay friends with Sam? (By writing more letters.)

Go through the story once more with your child. Then close the book. Ask your child to tell the story to you in his or her own words.

Reading Between the Lines

Talk to your child about why the dolls were worried when Sam Lamb moved away—they thought they were losing a friend. How did Sam Lamb feel when he left? (He was sad and probably a little frightened.) Discuss how the dolls planned to remain friends with Sam Lamb by writing letters to him.

Your Child and a Friend Moving Away

Ask your child to describe what a friend is. The descriptions will vary with each child. Some possible answers: "A friend is somebody I like and who likes me" and "A friend is somebody who knows I like to play with trucks."

Talk it over. What would happen if your child's close friend (rather than a playground acquaintance) moved away? How would your child feel? Point out that friendships can be kept up in many ways—by letters, phone calls, even visits.

Though the emphasis is on keeping up friendships, you have to be realistic. The friend who has left may not respond or, after an initial flurry of letters and calls, the friendship may fade away.

Grow-and-Learn Activities

Drawing a Friend Have your child draw a pic-ture of his or her best friend. Help by writing the friend's name at the top of the page and My Best Friend at the bottom. Display this picture in a special place. As a different drawing activity, you might help your child and a friend draw tracings of each other's hands. The children can save the drawings as keepsakes.

Communication Help your child write a let-ter to his or her best friend. As your child dictates the letter, you can write the words. It need not be a long letter, and you can leave plenty of space around the edges for your child to add artwork. Show your child how to put the letter into an envelope, seal it, address it, and place a stamp on it. Allow your child to give the letter to the postal carrier or drop it in the mailbox.

Friend's Day Try to arrange a special day of activities for your child and his or her best friend. This day can be spent at home, quietly drawing pictures and having a snack, or something more elaborate can be planned, such as a trip to a museum or the circus. If possible, take several photographs that both children can put in scrap-books. These scrapbooks can be labeled Friends and added to over time.

Grow-and-Learn Library

Raggedy Ann and Andy's Grow-and-Learn Library has books with two themes that are similar to *Sam Lamb Moves Away. The Jack-in-the-Box* (Volume 11) explores making new friends. *The Sleepover* (Volume 16) is about sleeping away from home.

RAGGEDY DOG TO THE RESCUE

About the Story

Raggedy Dog feels left out when the other dolls
make a fuss over a newcomer, Raggedy Cat. Raggedy
Dog constantly suspects Raggedy Cat's motives for being
kind and generous. When he thinks Raggedy Cat is taking his
ball, Raggedy Dog becomes furious. He chases the cat all the way
to Raggedy Land and up a tree. But, realizing what he has done,
Raggedy Dog goes to heroic measures to rescue Raggedy Cat.
They become fast friends.

About the Theme

Raggedy Dog to the Rescue is a model story
about jealousy. Children often experience this emotion
—whether it is because of a new baby in the family,
a friend who has a bigger bicycle, or a playmate with a newer toy.
Reading and discussing this story will help your child to recognize
and deal with many types of jealousy.

Reading the Story

As you read this story, have your child sit with you so you can both enjoy the pictures. When your child is familiar with the story, you can ask questions such as the following.

    1. Why was Raggedy Dog upset? (Because everybody was paying more attention to Raggedy Cat.)

    2. Why did Raggedy Dog chase Raggedy Cat? (Because he thought she had taken his ball.)

    3. How far did Raggedy Dog chase Raggedy Cat? (All the way to Raggedy Land.)

    4. What is special about pincushion trees? (They are planted in pots, not in the ground.)

    5. Who slept in Raggedy Dog's bed that night? (Raggedy Dog and Raggedy Cat.)

When your child can accurately answer these and other questions about the story, ask him or her to retell the story, using the pictures in the book to help maintain the correct sequence.

Reading Between the Lines

Ask your child to tell you how Raggedy Dog felt about Raggedy Cat at the beginning of the story. Tell your child that the name for this feeling is *jealousy*. Ask if Raggedy Dog was right to feel this way. (No. He had no reason to be jealous of Raggedy Cat.) Why? (His friends loved him as much as they had before Raggedy Cat came to live with them.) Have your child explain how Raggedy Cat must have felt about being chased out of the playroom. Finally, talk about how much better Raggedy Dog felt after he began to help care for Raggedy Cat.

Your Child and Jealousy

Ask if your child has ever felt jealous of another person. What was the reason? Point out that jealousy is not a good feeling. It makes the jealous person unhappy. If your child is jealous of another person, such as a sister or brother, encourage an honest talk about the reasons for this jealousy. Your child probably needs some gentle reinforcement of being loved, wanted, and considered special.

    Refer to Volume 1, *Sunny Bunny Comes Home*, for activities that help your child feel special.

Grow-and-Learn Activities

Wish Book Help your child make a Wish Book. Staple together several blank sheets of paper along one edge. Help write your child's name and Wish Book on the front cover. Pictures of things your child would like to have can be cut out and pasted in the book. The pictures, which can be hand-drawn or taken from magazines or catalogues, can range from an elephant to a new dress.

Wish Book II Help your child make a second Wish Book. This one should contain pictures of things your child wishes to give others or help others do. Both books may be helpful at birthday or holiday time.

Learning About Cats Your child may enjoy learning about cats. Your local library will probably have picture books about cats. Many pet stores allow children to handle and play with kittens. If your family has a cat, your child might like to make sure it has food, water, and toys.

Grow-and-Learn Library

Read more about Raggedy Dog in Volume 10, *Raggedy Dog's Bone*, and Volume 14, *Raggedy Dog Learns to Share*.

VOLUME 5

WHAT CAN A CAMEL DO?

About the Story

At the talent show in Raggedy Land, all the dolls in the playroom are invited to demonstrate their special talents. They immediately begin to practice, but The Camel with the Wrinkled Knees can't think of a thing to do. He tries to imitate the others, but fails. When the dolls can't convey their equipment to the show, The Camel realizes what *he* can do. He can carry everything to the show! The Camel is proud of his special talent— and so are his playroom friends!

About the Theme

What Can a Camel Do? illustrates the theme everyone can do something special. Everyone has a talent, whether it's drawing beautiful pictures, being a good listener, or being a fast runner. This story will help your child realize that he or she also can do something special.

Reading the Story

Read the story aloud to your child. Talk about the meaning of the word *talent*—the ability to do something special. When you've read and discussed the story, ask questions such as the following:

1. What is Percy the Policeman's special talent? (Playing a tune on his policeman's whistle.)

2. What is Raggedy Andy's special talent? (Turning somersaults.)

3. What is Greta the Dutch Doll's special talent? (Doing a dance.)

4. What special talent did The Camel with the Wrinkled Knees discover he had? (Being able to carry many things.)

5. What prize did the dolls give The Camel? (A badge for being a helpful friend.)

Ask your child to retell the story. Provide guidance in presenting the story in sequence.

Reading Between the Lines

Ask your child to tell you what The Camel with the Wrinkled Knees learned in the story (that everyone can do something special). Help your child understand that even though two people may know how to do the same thing, they always do it a little differently from each other, in their own special way.

Your Child's Special Talents

Encourage your child to name some special things that he or she can do. These can range from being a good jumper to being able to hide in a small space under the bed to making a unique silly face.

Talk about some of the special things that family members can do. Grandma may bake the best cookies in the world, or an older sister may ice skate well. Talk about what your child's friends do that makes them special, too.

Grow-and-Learn Activities

What I Can Do Help your child make a poster. Take a large sheet of paper and fold it in half both ways. Have your child draw a line along the folds, dividing the paper into four parts. In four separate pictures, have your child draw some of the things that make him or her special. When each picture is complete, write an appropriate title underneath it. Display the poster in a prominent place.

Special Interests Find a large piece of heavy cardboard. Ask your child to name a favorite sport or activity. (It may be something the child has done or would simply like to do.) Write this subject at the top of the cardboard. Allow your child to look through several old magazines and cut out pictures of people involved in this activity. Have your child paste the pictures on the cardboard. This can lead to a discussion of how each person pictured is doing something different and special.

Dramatization Ask your child first to act out how Greta danced and then how The Camel danced. Greta should be more graceful and coordinated, while The Camel is very likely to trip over his own feet and fall down. This exercise can be repeated with Sunny Bunny's hopping and, depending on your child's ability, Raggedy Andy's somersaults.

Grow-and-Learn Library

For more about being special, your child will enjoy *Sunny Bunny Comes Home* (Volume 1). Additional examples of unique talents can be found in Volume 15, *Raggedy Andy's Perfect Party*.

BABETTE'S SCARY NIGHT

About the Story

When Marcella's parents take her camping for the weekend, the dolls decide to camp out in the backyard playhouse. But Babette is reluctant to join them since she's afraid of the dark. As night approaches and the playhouse grows dark, the dolls begin to tell a round-robin story. Babette imagines that the story is coming true and jumps at every shadow and noise. But the others show her that she really has nothing to fear. By the end of the story, Babette is just as unafraid of the dark as the other dolls.

About the Theme

Babette's Scary Night is about fear of the dark. In the dark, common noises take on awful meanings and shadows seem to take on lives of their own. Babette's imagination, like many children's, creates terrifying monsters that are simply not there. Reading and talking about this story will help your child understand that darkness is only frightening when imaginations take over.

Reading the Story

Read the story aloud, encouraging your child to point out the action and characters in the pictures. Ask the following questions to be sure your child understands the story.

   1. Where did the dolls camp out? (In the playhouse.)
   2. Why did Babette want to stay in the playroom? (Because she was afraid of staying outside in the dark.)
   3. Who began to tell the story? (Sunny Bunny.)
   4. What was the real cause of the scratching noise at the door? (Raggedy Dog and Raggedy Cat.)
   5. What broke the wizard's spell over the animals? (The fact that the children weren't afraid.)

Reading Between the Lines

Help your child understand that Babette was afraid of the dark because she imagined that scary things were happening. As her imagination took over, her fears multiplied. When the other dolls showed Babette that there was really nothing to fear in the dark, she learned to be brave and had a good time camping out after all.

Your Child and the Dark

If your child is afraid of the dark, it might help to sit in a darkened room with him or her, listening to soothing music and recalling pleasant times with family and friends. Point out that although it seems very dark when the light first goes out, our eyes quickly adjust and we begin to see the familiar objects in the room. Plan a night tour of your home with the lights out. (You might point out a favorite object, such as a chair or toy chest, and

talk about whether it looks different or the same.) If the moon is shining, have fun making shadow pictures on a wall.

Grow-and-Learn Activities

Dramatization Ask your child to act out the part of Babette as you reread the story. At first Babette is reluctant to leave the playroom, then afraid of the noises in the dark, and finally very brave. As you read, encourage your child to supply some of the sound effects, such as the scraping at the door and the screeching of the owl.

   What's That Sound? Play a sound identification game with your child. Have your child close his or her eyes. Make a simple noise, such as the closing of a squeaky door, a ringing doorbell, or feet walking up or down steps. Ask your child to identify the sound.

   Camping Out If possible, build a tent in the backyard (the living room will do) by hanging a blanket over four chairs arranged in a circle. Allow your child to pretend to camp out. Explain that camping out means roughing it—no television, no kitchen, and no electric lights.

Grow-and-Learn Library

The fear of the dark theme is similar to "sleeping away from home," which is illustrated in *The Sleepover* (Volume 16).

A VERY CLOSE CALL

About the Story

The dolls decide to play a game of hide-and-seek, and Raggedy Ann volunteers to be It. Bubbles the Clown hides in the pantry, but the wind blows the door securely shut, and Bubbles can't reach the doorknob. After all the others are found, Bubbles calls for help so that he can get back to the playroom before Marcella returns home. The dolls work together at the difficult task of opening so large a door. Their cooperation and repeated efforts pay off, and Bubbles is released just in time.

About the Theme

The theme of *A Very Close Call* is try, try again. If one solution to a problem fails, think up another one. If that solution doesn't work, try another and another. The important thing is to keep trying. Reading and discussing this story with your child will help him or her understand the benefits of trying over and over.

Reading the Story

Read *A Very Close Call* with your child. Talk about what is happening in the pictures. Ask your child questions such as the following to assure understanding of the story.

1. What game did the dolls play? (Hide and seek.)

2. Who was It? (Raggedy Ann.)

3. Where did Raggedy Andy hide? (Behind the clock.)

4. Why couldn't Bubbles get out of the pantry? (The wind had blown the door tightly shut.)

5. How did the dolls get the door open? (Percy the Policeman lassoed the handle, Raggedy Andy climbed up the broom to turn the handle, and the others pulled on the rope.)

After your child has become familiar with the story, have him or her retell it. Let your child handle the book and turn the pages as he or she ''reads.''

Reading Between the Lines

Ask your child to tell you what might have happened if the dolls had given up trying after they were unable to move the chair. (Marcella might have found Bubbles in the pantry, instead of the playroom.) Explain that one shouldn't give up just because a problem isn't solved on the first try, but that it is better to try again.

Your Child and Trying Again

Encourage your child to tell you about a difficult problem that led to trying several different solutions. This might be something such as learning to tie shoelaces or retrieving a toy from a hard-to-reach spot under a sofa. Point out that even star athletes have to practice repeatedly in order to get things right.

Talk with your child about some things that may be difficult to do, such as buttoning a sweater or putting a puzzle together. Go over these activities with your child and look for new ways to do them or to remember how they are done. Encourage your child to be creative in solving the problems.

Grow-and-Learn Activities

Fire Escape This is a thinking game you can play with your child. Explain that if there is a fire in your home, the first thing he or she must do is get out of the house safely—or *escape*. Then give your child the location of an imaginary fire, and ask how he or she would escape safely. Vary the place of the fire, so that your child must come up with new ideas. This is also a good time to discuss other rules of fire safety, such as never playing with matches.

Hide and Seek Arrange for your child to play Hide and Seek with family members or friends. Stress the importance of finding a safe place to hide, getting completely out of sight, and keeping very quiet to avoid detection. Help your child learn to take turns being It and to carefully consider how to go about finding the others.

Goal Chart Set up a chart of four or five daily goals for your child, such as taking a bath or getting dressed independently, or feeding the dog without being reminded. These should be fairly easy tasks—things your child is entirely capable of doing but has a tendency to forget or ignore. Each day, as your child completes one of the activities, place a sticker or draw a star in the appropriate space on the chart. The first day that your child does all the activities well and without assistance, you might celebrate in a special way.

Grow-and-Learn Library

A different, yet parallel, story focusing on the theme you can help yourself is found in Volume 18, *Bubbles Goes to the Fair*. The themes try, try again and you can help yourself will work well together in a discussion with your child.

GROUCHY BEAR'S PARADE

About the Story

Marcella gets to choose a new toy at the toy store. She selects a teddy bear whom she calls Grouchy and takes him home to meet the other dolls in her playroom. Grouchy Bear would like to join in the playroom fun but feels obliged to live up to his new name. When the dolls are invited to a Teddy Bear Parade, Grouchy Bear wants to join in the fun and finds it even harder to remain grumpy. Raggedy Ann helps Grouchy Bear understand that it is acceptable to show others his true feelings. Grouchy Bear smiles so wonderfully that he is selected to lead the Teddy Bear Parade!

About the Theme

Grouchy Bear's Parade develops the theme show how you feel. Just because Marcella thinks the teddy bear looks grouchy, he believes he must hide his true feelings and act grouchy all the time. From reading and discussing this book, your child will learn that it is perfectly all right to reveal genuine feelings to other people.

Reading the Story

As you read *Grouchy Bear's Parade*, have your child point out the characters and activities in the pictures. Then ask questions such as the following so you can judge his or her comprehension of the story.

1. Where did Grouchy Bear get his name? (From Marcella.)

2. Why did Grouchy Bear act grumpy? (Because he thought Marcella wanted him to behave that way.)

3. How did Grouchy Bear help the baby sparrow? (By helping her to return to her nest in the tree.)

4. What old friend did Grouchy Bear meet at the Teddy Bear Parade? (The ballerina doll from the Town Toy Store.)

5. Why was Grouchy Bear picked to lead the parade? (Because he was a happy-looking bear.)

Reading Between the Lines

Ask your child to tell what Grouchy Bear learned from the sparrow and Raggedy Ann. (That it is okay to be happy sometimes and sad sometimes, and it's okay to show how you really feel. Point out that, by pretending to be grumpy, Grouchy Bear had missed a lot of fun in the playroom.

Your Child and Feelings

Talk to your child about some activities that make him or her feel happy (being allowed to stay up late) or sad (losing a favorite toy or book). Point out that there are acceptable ways for people to show how they feel about certain things. For example, happy feelings are commonly displayed through smiles, hugs, or bubbly demonstrations, but leaping and cavorting around the room may be dangerous and upsetting. Unhappy feelings might be expressed through frowns, sad faces, or quietly asking for help; screaming and kicking don't usually help solve a problem or make an unhappy person feel better.

Grow-and-Learn Activities

The Grump In this game, one player is The Grump and must wear a deep, dark frown. The other player tries to force The Grump to smile by telling jokes or making silly faces. Once The Grump smiles, the players switch roles.

Happy/Sad Poster Help your child make a happy/sad poster for the door of his or her room. On one side of a piece of paper, have your child draw a self-portrait of a happy face, and on the other side, a self-portrait of a sad face. Your child can select which side of the poster is showing according to how he or she is feeling.

Dramatization Have your child act out the part of Grumpy Bear as you once again read the story. Remind your child that many times Grumpy Bear wanted to smile but felt he shouldn't. An oversized winter coat (possibly from an older brother or sister) may give your child the feeling of being a round, puffy, stuffed teddy bear.

Grow-and-Learn Library

The theme of this story, show how you feel, can be reinforced by reading Volume 10, *Raggedy Dog's Bone*, which deals with honesty. For other examples of learning to cope with feelings, read *Babette's Scary Night* (Volume 6), or *Little Bear's Problem* (Volume 2).

THE BOX OF TRICKS

About the Story

Marcella receives many wonderful presents for her birthday.
Among them is a box of tricks, which fascinates Raggedy Andy. As
soon as he is able, he investigates the box and discovers
several interesting tricks. He begins to play these tricks on his friends
as practical jokes, but they are not very nice tricks and his
friends do not appreciate the fun. Raggedy Andy stops only after
the tables are turned and a trick is played on him.
That's when he finally learns that teasing is
not a nice thing to do!

About the Theme

The Box of Tricks shows that teasing is not a pleasant matter.
Whether is takes the form of a simple trick such as paper snakes
popping out of a can or is something much more severe
such as name-calling or personal slurs, teasing remains
a potentially vicious activity. By reading and discussing this story
with your child, you can demonstrate that teasing is something to
be avoided, especially when it harms the victims.

Reading the Story

Read *The Box of Tricks* with your child. Discuss what is happening in the pictures. Have your child answer questions such as the following.

1. Where did the box of tricks come from? (Marcella got it for her birthday.)

2. What trick did Raggedy Andy play on Babette? (Taking her picture with a camera that squirted water.)

3. What trick did Raggedy Andy play on Raggedy Dog? (Jerking the string when Raggedy Dog tried to get the bone.)

4. What trick did Raggedy Andy play on Sunny Bunny? (Sprinkling sneezing powder near him.)

5. What trick did Raggedy Andy play on himself? (Causing fake snakes to jump out of the can.)

Reading Between the Lines

Ask your child to tell what Raggedy Andy learned in the story. (That tricks often are not funny to the person they're played on.) Teasing can hurt a person deeply. Have your child describe how Babette and Raggedy Dog must have felt after they had been tricked. Point out that Raggedy Andy couldn't understand how they felt until one of his own tricks backfired and scared him.

Your Child and Teasing

Ask if your child has ever played a trick on or teased another child. Help him or her to imagine how that other child must have felt. If your child has ever been tricked or teased, discuss the feelings that result from such treatment. Point out that what is funny to one person may not be funny to another.

Have your child think up several reasons that tricks should not be played on another person. Answers might include ''Because it's embarrassing'' or ''Because it hurts.'' Emphasize that planning helpful surprises is an acceptable alternative to playing tricks.

Grow-and-Learn Activities

Surprise! Help your child think of helpful ways to surprise another member of the family or a neighbor. (For example, setting the table, taking a home-made picture or treat to an elderly shut-in, or volunteering to play with a younger brother or sister.) Then, you and your child can decide how to carry out the plan.

Secret Pen Pal As another positive surprise, you might help your child write an unsigned letter to send to a friend or relative. This could be a drawing without words, or perhaps your child would enjoy printing a simple message on it, with your assistance. If the letter goes to another adult, you may want to arrange to have that person talk to your child about the wonderful surprise and how good it feels to be remembered.

Grab Bag Place several objects, such as a block, a crayon, a cup, and a comb, in a deep box or in a bag. Without looking, have your child reach in, select an object, and guess what it is by feeling its shape.

Grow-and-Learn Library

Surprises aren't always unpleasant—share a positive view with your child by reading Volume 17, *The Birthday Surprise*.

RAGGEDY DOG'S BONE

About the Story

More than anything else in the world, Raggedy Dog
would like to have a real dog bone. He can't
believe his luck when he finally finds one in a pile of
dirt in the backyard. Later, Fido (Marcella's real dog)
explains to Raggedy Dog that *he* had buried a bone and
now can't find it. Fido is very sad. Raggedy Dog, realizing
that it's best to be honest, returns Fido's bone.
Fido understands how Raggedy Dog
feels and offers to share the bone with him.
Both dogs are very happy!

About the Theme

The theme of *Raggedy Dog's Bone* is honesty.
By being honest, Raggedy Dog made a new friend in Fido.
He also avoided feeling guilty about depriving Fido
of his very own bone. Reading and discussing the story
with your child can lead to an understanding
that honesty is right in any set of circumstances.

Reading the Story

Read *Raggedy Dog's Bone* aloud with your child. Allow time to discuss each of the pictures. Ask questions such as the following to assure understanding of the story.

1. Where did Raggedy Dog look for a bone? (In the toybox, the toolshed, and under the porch.)

2. Where did Raggedy Dog find a bone? (In a pile of dirt.)

3. Where did Raggedy Dog hide the bone from Fido? (Behind the apple tree.)

4. How did Raggedy Dog know it was Fido's bone? (Because Fido told Raggedy Dog that he had buried the bone right where Raggedy Dog found it.)

5. How did Fido make Raggedy Dog happy? (By sharing the bone with him.)

Reading Between the Lines

Ask your child to describe what Raggedy Dog learned in the story. (That being honest can make both himself and others happy.) Have your child imagine how Fido might have felt if Raggedy Dog had kept the bone. How would Raggedy Dog have felt toward Fido? By being honest, Raggedy Dog made Fido and himself very happy.

Your Child and Being Honest

Talk with your child about some examples of honesty: returning a dropped coin to its proper owner, admitting to the breakage of an item, or simply by following household rules without being reminded. Discuss openly the many feelings that can result from honest behavior—pride, relief, or even anxiety.

You may also want to discuss the results of dishonest behavior. Children might be punished—sent to their rooms or not be allowed to watch television. For serious offenses, adults might be sent to jail. Be sure to point out that the best reward for being honest is feeling good about oneself.

Grow-and-Learn Activities

Dramatization Ask your child to play the part of Raggedy Dog as he looks for a bone. Point out that since Raggedy Dog doesn't really know where bones come from, he looks everywhere. Encourage your child to get down on hands and knees in order to look at things from a dog's perspective.

Model Clay Dogs Your child will enjoy making model dogs from clay or play dough. You can either use store-bought play dough or make your own using the following recipe:

1 cup flour
1/3 cup salt
1/3 to 1/2 cup water

Mix the dry ingredients. Stir in the water a little at a time, using only enough to make a dough of modeling consistency. Allow project to air-dry for one day. For colored dough, add food coloring into the mixture with the water.

Visit the Pet Store All children love to visit pet stores. You might take your child on a just-for browsing field trip to a local pet store. Point out the many different breeds of dogs: some are small, some large, some short-haired, some long-haired. Allow your child to talk to a pet store worker about the proper way to take care of a dog. Many pet stores have Puppy Play Pens, where your child can actually play with a puppy. If you already have a dog in your household, encourage your child to help take care of it.

Grow-and-Learn Library

Your child can join Raggedy Dog for more adventures in Volume 4, *Raggedy Dog to the Rescue* and Volume 14, *Raggedy Dog Learns to Share*.

THE JACK-IN-THE-BOX

About the Story

Marcella's cousin David brings a Jack-in-the-Box with him when he comes to visit. The other dolls discover that the box can make pretty music. But Jack, who lives in the box, doesn't want to play. The dolls continue with their pretend circus, and Jack is overcome with curiosity. When the dolls see Jack peeking out of his box, they again invite him to join in the fun. Jack's music is perfect for their circus. Jack and the dolls become friends!

About the Theme

The Jack-in-the-Box investigates what can happen in the course of making new friends. Jack hides his shyness with a bit of bragging and arrogance. His situation is similar to that of a child on the first day of school—being shy and unsure of oneself among strangers is quite natural. Sharing this story will open your child's eyes to the wonderful possibilities of making new friends.

Reading the Story

After you have read *The Jack-in-the-Box*, ask questions such as the following to be sure your child understands the story.

1. Who brought The Jack-in-the-Box to the playroom? (Marcella's cousin David.)

2. What can The Jack-in-the-Box do? (Play music.)

3. What did the dolls do when Jack went back in his box? (Played circus.)

4. Why did Jack go back in his box at first? (Because he didn't want to play.)

5. Why did Jack come out of his box? (Because the dolls were having a good time, and he wanted to play, too.)

Allow your child to have some private time with the book. Later, ask him or her to retell the story with the events in the correct order.

Reading Between the Lines

Ask your child to explain how Jack felt when he first arrived in the playroom. (He may have felt frightened or insecure among strangers.) Talk about what would have happened if Jack had remained in his box. (He would not have made friends with the other dolls.) Although making new friends can be scary, it is worth the risk.

Your Child and Making New Friends

Ask your child if he or she has ever felt as Jack did in the story. This feeling could stem from being introduced to a large number of new people in an unfamiliar situation, such as the first day of school, or from having a group of strangers come into the home, as when an older sibling has friends over. Explain that it is natural to feel a little shy when we first meet someone.

Ask your child to recall the first meeting with his or her closest friend. Was it very easy, or was it hard at first? No matter how the two met, they are now best friends!

Grow-and-Learn Activities

Playing Jack-in-the-Box Have your child pretend to be a Jack-in-the-Box hiding behind a chair or table. You can hum or sing. When you stop singing, your child should jump up. (You can also use a radio or cassette player.) Vary the lengths of the tunes from very short to very long, so that your child will have to pay attention.

Making a New Friend The next time your child asks to invite a friend over to play, suggest that he or she ask a new friend to come over. Remind your child how The-Jack-in-the-Box felt, and explain that the new friend must be made to feel welcome.

Making a Jack-in-the-Box You can help your child make a non-working Jack-in-the-Box. The box can be made from an old square tissue box covered with colored paper or fabric. The Jack can be made from a styrofoam ball and scraps of yarn, fabric, and paper. Encourage your child to draw a happy face on the Jack-in-the-Box, using magic markers or gluing on buttons and other notions.

Grow-and-Learn Library

For a different perspective of the same situation, refer to Volume 3, *Sam Lamb Moves Away*, which focuses on a friend's moving away. The entire cast of characters in the playroom will be found together again in Volume 13, *The Play in the Attic*.

VOLUME 12
PLAY BALL!

About the Story

Raggedy Ann and Raggedy Andy visit the dolls at
the home of Marcella's cousin David and are invited to
play in a baseball game. Raggedy Ann shows ability to hit the ball.
Raggedy Andy can pitch, but he can't hit very well.
When Raggedy Andy finally gets a hit in the last inning of the game,
he is so excited that he forgets to run around the bases. Instead,
he is easily tagged out, and his team loses. In spite of the outcome
of the game, the members of both teams remain friends.

About the Theme

Play Ball! highlights the theme of sportsmanship.
Even though there was fierce competition on the
field during the game, once the game is over there
are no hard feelings and the friendships remain
intact. Reading and discussing the story can help your child
understand the meaning of sportsmanship: winning *and* losing
gracefully and not allowing the results to interfere with friendships.

Reading the Story

Read *Play Ball*! with your child. Afterward, ask questions such as the following to be sure he or she understands the story.

1. Where did Marcella take Raggedy Ann and Raggedy Andy? (To her cousin David's house.)

2. Why were the dolls in David's room making grumpy faces at each other? (Because they were going to play against each other in a baseball game.)

3. What could Raggedy Ann do well? (Hit the ball.)

4. What could Raggedy Andy do well? (Throw the ball.)

5. What did Raggedy Andy forget to do after he hit the ball? (Run around the bases.)

Have your child turn the pages of the book and "read" the story to you. Encourage him or her to maintain the correct sequence of events.

Reading Between the Lines

Help your child recall what happened at the very end of the story (all the dolls were friends once again). Point out that Hank Homer admired Raggedy Andy because he tried so hard, and that all the dolls had enjoyed playing the game. It didn't matter to them who had won, as long as everybody played their best and had a good time. Explain to your child that the word for this is sportsmanship—losing and winning gracefully.

Your Child and Sportsmanship

Ask your child to name a game that he or she likes to play with a best friend. How does winning make your child feel? How does losing make your child feel? Point out that in spite of winning or losing, the other child remains a best friend. That is sportsmanship.

You might point out other examples of sportsmanship when you are watching TV or reading magazines or newspapers. After many professional sports events, the players from opposing teams will shake hands.

Grow-and-Learn Activities

Friends Picture Fold a large piece of paper in thirds. Help your child draw lines on the folds to divide the paper. Ask him or her to draw three pictures—how it feels to win, how it feels to lose, and how it feels to be with a best friend. When the drawing is complete, write "Winning," "Losing," and "Best Friends" at the top of the appropriate pictures, and display them.

A New Game Encourage your child and a friend to learn how to play a new game. This can be a store-bought game or something as simple as "I Spy." Help them learn the rules, and remind them to practice good sportsmanship. Offer to act as referee if any question or controversy arises.

Baseball Game Attend a baseball game with your child. It can be a major-league game, a high-school game, or just an informal game among friends on a weekend. Since the basic rules of the game are simple, you should be able to answer most of your child's questions. You might encourage him or her to bring along a friend.

Grow-and-Learn Library

To extend the theme of sportsmanship, refer to Volume 14, *Raggedy Dog Learns to Share*, and Volume 15, *Raggedy Andy's Perfect Party*.

THE PLAY IN THE ATTIC

About the Story

All the dolls are taken to the attic while Marcella's playroom is being painted. At first they are upset that their plans for an exciting night have been ruined. As they search through some old trunks, Raggedy Ann suggests that they put on a play. The dolls all help to stage "Goldilocks and the Three Bears," either acting or working behind the scenes. They finally realize that they have had a wonderful time making the most of an unplanned trip to the attic.

About the Theme

The Play in the Attic demonstrates the theme of making the best of things. Even though plans are sometimes changed due to uncontrollable circumstances, it is still possible to have a good time. Your child will enjoy reading and discussing this story with you and learning how to make the best of things.

Reading the Story

Read *The Play in the Attic* with your child. Have him or her point out the different characters and explain what each is doing in the pictures. Pose questions such as the following to assure your child's understanding of the story.

1. What did Raggedy Andy plan to do that night? (Start a pillow fight.)
2. Why did the dolls have to go to the attic? (Because Marcella's playroom was being painted.)
3. What story did the dolls decide to act out? (The story of "Goldilocks and the Three Bears.")
4. Who played the part of Goldilocks? (Babette the French Doll.)
5. Who told the story? (Raggedy Ann.)

Allow your child to look through the book independently. Then ask him or her to retell the story.

Reading Between the Lines

Ask your child to tell you what the dolls learned that first night in the attic (that they could still have a good time, even if they weren't where they had planned to be). Sometimes the most careful plans have to be put aside when something unexpected happens. Those who make the best of a situation will have the most fun.

Your Child and Making the Best of Things

Your child should be able to recall a time when expectations were dashed because of unforeseen complications. Perhaps a picnic had to be cancelled due to rain, or a visit cancelled due to illness. Help your child recall what replaced the original activity. Did your child have a good time by making the best of things?

Help your child recall other times when plans had to be changed. How did he or she make the best of things in these situations?

Grow-and-Learn Activities

Dramatization Have your child and several of his or her friends act out the story of *Goldilocks and the Three Bears*. Allow each child to select a character to portray as you read the story aloud. If they practice a few times, you might invite other parents and children to watch the final performance.

My Very Own Story Ask your child to make up a story called The Bear and the Three Goldilocks. Ask your child to first think about the story and then to draw four or five pictures that will help him or her tell it. Arrange a special time when your child can tell you the story. Write the story down and staple the pages together to form a book of your child's very own.

A Real Play Your child might enjoy seeing a real play. This can range from a high school play, to a Children's Theater performance, to a professional production. Be sure to select a production on a level your child will comprehend. Talk about the play afterwards. Did your child like the story? Who was the hero? Compare the play to a movie or television.

Grow-and-Learn Library

All the residents of the playroom can be found in Volume 11, *The Jack-in-the-Box*. A theme similar to the one in this story is you can help yourself, discussed in Volume 18, *Bubbles Goes to the Fair*.

RAGGEDY DOG LEARNS TO SHARE

About the Story

Fido, Marcella's real dog, is Raggedy Dog's hero. When
Fido leaves his ball in the playroom for
Raggedy Dog to play with, Raggedy Dog refuses to let
any of the other dolls play with it at all. But the
ball does not roll around or bounce high for Raggedy
Dog the same way it does for Fido. Raggedy Dog finally
realizes that it takes more than one to play fetch or catch.
He apologizes to the others for being selfish,
and they all take turns throwing the ball.
The game is so much more exciting when everyone can share!

About the Theme

Raggedy Dog Learns to Share is about sharing. The ball turns
out to be useless without someone to throw it and
someone else to catch it. To help your child understand the
good feelings that come from sharing, read and then
discuss this story together.

Reading the Story

When you read *Raggedy Dog Learns to Share*, ask your child to point out the events and characters in the story. After your child is familiar with the story, ask questions such as the following.

1. How did Raggedy Dog get Fido's ball? (Fido left it for him to play with.)

2. What did the other dolls want to do with the ball? (Play catch.)

3. What did the ball do when Raggedy Dog played with it? (Nothing.)

4. Who showed Raggedy Dog that it took more than one to play with the ball? (The Camel with the Wrinkled Knees.)

5. When did Raggedy Dog have fun with the ball? (When he was sharing it with all the other dolls.)

Ask your child to retell the story in his or her own words. Use the book as reference to make sure the sequence is correct.

Reading Between the Lines

Ask your child to tell you what Raggedy Dog learned in the story. (That sharing adds to the fun of every activity.) Raggedy Dog couldn't have fun with the ball until he shared it with his friends. Discuss how the other dolls felt when Raggedy Dog would not share with them. (They felt hurt.) Remind your child that sharing enabled everyone to have fun!

Your Child and Sharing

Ask your child to think of other situations in which sharing is important. Most simple games are not enjoyable if only one person plays. Sharing can involve taking turns (on a swing), dividing something (a popsicle), or joining in a group (playing a game).

Talk about your child's own sharing experiences. How did it feel to share? What might the other person have felt if your child had not shared? Be sure to compliment your child for sharing.

Grow-and-Learn Activities

Share a Toy Help your child look through his or her toys, books, or clothing to find some that are no longer used. Who might enjoy borrowing or receiving one of these as a gift? (Set aside any that you want to keep.) Encourage your child to think about sharing with a brother, sister, cousin, friend, neighbor, or an unknown child who can receive charitable donations.

Tea Time Help your child plan a small informal tea party for one or two friends. Work together to bake cookies, choose pretty napkins, and set the table. Since anticipation is part of the fun, schedule the party a week or two in advance. Work together to create and send invitations.

Two-Person Drawing You and your child can share a fun time by taking turns adding details to a picture. Start by drawing a large circle on a piece of paper. Ask your child to think of what it can be and then add one part to the picture. For example, he or she might decide to make a face and add a nose. You add a detail, such as one eye, and then it's your child's turn again. Continue until you are both satisfied that the picture is finished. You might want to label the picture at the top and write *Our Picture* and both of your names at the bottom.

Grow-and-Learn-Library

For themes that complement the one in this story, refer to Volume 12, *Play Ball!*, which discusses sportsmanship, and Volume 15, *Raggedy Andy's Perfect Party*, which discusses cooperation.

RAGGEDY ANDY'S PERFECT PARTY

About the Story

Raggedy Andy suggests that the dolls celebrate the first day of summer by having a party. The others consider this an excellent idea. The chores are written down and each is assigned to one of the dolls. Preparation proceeds smoothly until Raggedy Andy discovers that nobody is in charge of decorations.

With the assistance of Daphne the Dinosaur, the decorations are put up just in time for a wonderful party!

About the Theme

Raggedy Andy's Perfect Party is about cooperation. No doll could have done all the work; all the dolls had to cooperate in order to do it. When you read and discuss this story, your child will learn some of the benefits of working well with other people.

Reading the Story

Read *Raggedy Andy's Perfect Party* with your child. Pause frequently to allow careful examination of the pictures. Ask questions such as the following to make sure your child understands the story.

1. Why are the dolls planning a party? (To celebrate the first day of summer.)
2. Who helped Raggedy Andy get ready for the party? (Babette, Percy, Tim, Sunny Bunny, Bubbles, Greta, Raggedy Ann, Raggedy Dog, Raggedy Cat, Tallyho, The Camel, and Daphne.)
3. What did Raggedy Andy forget? (The decorations.)
4. Why couldn't he hang the decorations himself? (Because the trees were too high for him to reach.)
5. How did Daphne help? (By letting Raggedy Andy climb up her back.)

Ask your child to retell the story in his or her own words. Encourage your child to keep the events in the correct order.

Reading Between the Lines

Ask your child to tell why Raggedy Andy's party was a success (because everybody pitched in and helped with the preparations). Have your child imagine what the party might have been like if nobody had helped Raggedy Andy (it probably would have been a shambles.) Point out that it was a wonderful party because everyone cooperated.

Your Child and Cooperation

Explain to your child that to cooperate means to work together. Ask your child to tell you about times he or she has been cooperative. Perhaps your child set the dinner table, helped to dry the dishes, or walked the dog. Be sure to praise your child for doing these things.

Ask your child to give other firsthand examples of cooperation. Your child may have noticed that drivers will take turns crossing at intersections or that many people work together to build a house.

Grow-and-Learn Activities

Cooperative Art Have your child and several friends or siblings paint a mural. This is most enjoyable (and won't cause a mess) when it is done outdoors. Unroll a length of brown or white shelf paper and tape the ends to a picnic table or a large flat board. Encourage the children to talk about what they would like to draw. Give them the freedom to do it their way. The children will discover that the project is more fun if they cooperate with each other.

More Cooperative Art Another enjoyable cooperative project for a group of children is a round-robin picture. Have the children sit around a table. Give each child a piece of paper. Ask the children to draw a funny face. Every few minutes, say "change!" The papers should now all be passed to the left. Each child then adds to the drawing that he or she receives. When the papers come back to the original position, the children can take turns displaying the finished products.

Family Reunion Have your child help plan a party for visiting family members. Ask your child to think of all the items that would be needed and write them in a list: How many chairs? How much food? Which activities? How long should the party last? Help your child decide who should be responsible for each item on the list.

Grow-and-Learn Library

Other examples of cooperation can be found in Volume 12, *Play Ball!*, Volume 14, *Raggedy Dog Learns to Share*, and Volume 17, *The Birthday Surprise*.

THE SLEEPOVER

About the Story

Marcella selects Sunny Bunny to go with her on an overnight visit to her friend Kathryn. While he is greatly honored, Sunny Bunny is worried about what Kathryn's playroom will be like and if her dolls will like him. Kathryn's dolls warmly welcome Sunny Bunny and they all teach each other how to play their favorite games. When he returns home, Sunny Bunny teaches the new games to his old friends. He realizes that sleeping away from home can be fun.

About the Theme

The Sleepover is about sleeping away from home. This can be a stressful experience for a child because familiar faces and surroundings are missing. But it's the perfect time to learn about and try new things. Reading and talking about the story can help your child realize the wonderful possibilities involved in spending the night in a new place.

Reading the Story

Read *The Sleepover* with your child and look at the pictures. Ask questions that will develop your child's understanding of the story. Examples might be:

1. Where did Marcella take Sunny Bunny? (To her friend Kathryn's house.)

2. Why was Sunny Bunny unhappy? (Because he missed his friends at home.)

3. What games did Kathryn's dolls teach Sunny Bunny? (London Bridge and Duck, Duck, Goose.)

4. What games did Sunny Bunny teach Kathryn's dolls? (Leap Frog and Hide-and-Seek.)

5. What did Sunny Bunny do when he got home? (Taught his friends to play the new games.)

Once your child has had some quiet time alone with the book and is familiar with the story, have him or her retell it.

Reading Between the Lines

How did Sunny Bunny feel when he first arrived at Kathryn's playroom? Explain that it is often scary to go to a new place. How did Sunny Bunny feel by the time he got home? (He had had a good time and was eager to show the others the new games he had learned.) Ask your child what might have happened if Sunny Bunny had become so scared that he didn't go (he would have missed meeting all his new friends and learning the new games).

Your Child and Sleeping Away from Home

If your child has slept away from home, have him or her describe what it was like. What happened at the new place? Was he or she homesick? Reassure your child that although it's okay to be homesick, being away from home can be a great adventure.

If your child has never slept away from home, ask him or her to imagine what it might be like to do so.

Grow-and-Learn Activities

Have a Friend Sleep Over Allow your child to invite a friend to spend the night. Have your child plan some activities for the evening. You might want to read *The Sleepover* to both children and talk about Sunny Bunny's feelings. Stress that sleeping over is a chance to learn new things. You may also want to have your child spend the night at a relative's home.

Travel Scrapbook Staple together several sheets of paper for a scrapbook. Allow your child to cut out magazine pictures of interesting places to visit and paste these pictures in the scrapbook. Challenge yourself too! Figure out the distance from your home to each place, and write it next to the picture. Talk with your child about how long it would take to get to each place and what might be found there.

Pack a Suitcase Pretend that your child is going on a trip, and help him or her pack a suitcase. Pick a destination for the imaginary trip. Discuss some basic items to include when packing, such as a toothbrush, a comb and brush, and pajamas. How many days will this trip take? Is the destination in a warm or cold climate? What will your child be doing at this place? The selection of clothes will depend on the climate and the intended activities.

Grow-and-Learn Library

Sleeping away from home is similar to the themes developed in Volume 2, *Little Bear's Problem*, and Volume 6, *Babette's Scary Night*.

THE BIRTHDAY SURPRISE

About the Story

While The Camel with the Wrinkled Knees is at the park with Marcella, the other dolls plan a birthday surprise for him. They decide to make him a birthday card, and Babette offers to pick a bouquet of flowers from the backyard. The dolls work long and hard to finish the card, but Babette spots a beautiful butterfly and forgets about the flowers. The dolls present their card to The Camel, who is delighted. Babette finally remembers the party and realizes that her friends were counting on her. She makes a bouquet of her own ribbons and presents it to The Camel. The dolls know they can depend on Babette.

About the Theme

The Birthday Surprise is about being dependable— you can depend on me. Everybody appreciates a person who is dependable, whether the occasion involves bringing bouquets, being on time, picking up toys, or being quiet at the right moment. Reading and discussing this story with your child can lead to an understanding of what it means to be dependable.

Reading the Story

Read *The Birthday Surprise* with your child. Have your child point out the characters in the pictures as you read aloud. Afterwards, ask your child questions about the story.

1. On what day does the story take place? (The Camel with the Wrinkled Knees' birthday.)

2. Where did Marcella take The Camel? (To the park.)

3. What did the other dolls plan to do for The Camel's birthday? (Make him a birthday card and give him a bouquet of flowers.)

4. Where did Babette go? (Chasing a butterfly into the meadow.)

5. What did Babette give The Camel? (A bouquet make out of ribbons.)

Reading Between the Lines

Ask your child what being dependable means (that people know you will do what you promised—that you are reliable). Was Babette dependable? (Not at first, but she came through at the end.) Have your child tell what he or she would have done in Babette's place when she spotted the butterfly and then when she realized there was no bouquet.

Your Child and Being Dependable

Ask your child to tell you some of the things you can depend on him or her to do. Answers might range from "Brushing my teeth every morning and night" to "Watering the plants every day" to "Going to bed on time."

Encourage your child to tell you some of the things he or she depends on others to do. Some answers might be "To do the laundry," or "To cook the food," or "To tell me a bedtime story." Ask your child to think about what might happen if the people doing these tasks were not dependable.

Grow-and-Learn Activities

Job Chart Talk about some of the jobs your child can do around the house. Make a chart of several of these jobs, using a small picture and a label to represent each job. For instance, the row for walking the dog might have a picture of a dog and the title Walk. Make an agreement with your child that he or she will promise to do these jobs and will be expected to carry them out. Your child can check off each job as it is done every day. Reward a completed chart!

Library Visit Visit your local library with your child. You can find many picture books that describe the work of community helpers, such as fire fighters, mail carriers, and police officers. Talk about each profession with your child. How are these people dependable?

Self-Portrait of the Future What does your child want to be when he or she grows up? (This may change from day to day.) Have your child draw a grown-up self-portrait. Discuss what is involved in your child's chosen job—who your child will depend on and who will depend on him or her in return. Label the picture with your child's name and future job title. Display the picture in a prominent place.

Grow-and-Learn Library

To enhance the theme you can depend on me, refer to Volume 15, *Raggedy Andy's Perfect Party*, which focuses on cooperation.

BUBBLES GOES TO THE FAIR

About the Story

The dolls are all preparing for the Raggedy Land Fair, especially Bubbles the Clown, who wants very much to win the juggling contest. He practices and practices. When the dolls arrive at the fair, Bubbles realizes that he has forgotten to bring his juggling balls. When he can find nobody to help him, Bubbles must either devise his own solution or miss the contest. He finally comes up with an idea. He borrows three apples, juggles the best he's ever juggled, and wins the contest!

About the Theme

Bubbles Goes to the Fair shows how you can help yourself. This can mean tying your own shoelaces, dressing yourself, finding something to do on a rainy day, or finding a substitute for balls to juggle with. Reading and discussing this story can help your child develop the ability to solve minor problems independently.

Reading the Story

Read *Bubbles Goes to the Fair* with your child. Have your child name the characters in the pictures and tell what is happening. Have your child answer questions such as the following to assure an understanding of the story.

1. Where was everybody going? (To the Raggedy Land Fair.)
2. What was Bubbles going to do at the fair? (Enter the juggling contest.)
3. How did Bubbles forget his juggling balls? (He put them down when he went back to get Sunny Bunny's rope.)
4. What did Bubbles use instead of three balls? (Three apples.)
5. Who won the juggling contest? (Bubbles the Clown.)

After becoming familiar with the story, your child should be able to retell it.

Reading Between the Lines

Ask your child to tell you what Bubbles learned in the story (that he did not always have to ask for help but could depend on himself for many things). Stress that there are times when it's better to ask for help, but it is often possible to solve small problems alone. Ask your child what might have happened if Bubbles had not thought of using the apples (chances are he would not have been in the contest).

Your Child and Helping Oneself

Has your child ever solved a problem independently? Examples: trying to play a game with one of the pieces missing or finding something to do on a rainy day. Point out that as your child gets older, he or she will be able to be more independent.

Explain that there are some times when a person must ask for help—in cases of emergency, illness, or fire, for example. Point out that there are people who are trained to help with serious problems.

Grow-and-Learn Activities

Things I Can Do Book Help your child make a book by stapling several sheets of paper together along one edge. Write Things I Can Do By Myself and your child's name on the front page. Have your child draw pictures of some of the things he or she can do without assistance, such as getting dressed alone, taking a bath, or pouring a glass of milk.

Matching Games Point out to your child that one aspect of helping oneself is learning to enjoy time alone. An easy game for younger children to play alone is *Old Maid*, a card matching game that can be purchased at most discount department stores. You can easily help your child learn an at-home variation of this game using dominoes or a standard card deck. The object of the game remains the same: pick matching pairs of cards or dominoes from a well-mixed pile.

Emergencies All children should know what to do in an emergency. If you have 911 service in your area, post the phone number in large numerals by the phone. Emphasize that it is to be used for emergencies only. If you do not have 911, make a list of numbers for the fire department, the police department, and a nearby relative or neighbor. Have your child help cut out appropriate pictures and write the phone numbers next to them.

Grow-and-Learn Library

A Very Close Call, which is Volume 7, has a similar theme of try, try, again.

TIM'S BIG ADVENTURE

About the Story

When a rainstorm ruins the dolls' chance to play outside,
they agree to listen to Raggedy Ann read a story.
But Tim the Toy Soldier is at first reluctant to listen.
When he does begin to listen, his imagination takes over.
Suddenly, he is sparring with dragons,
swimming in a castle moat, and rescuing Babette!
The book ends with Tim realizing that his imagination can provide
him with many great adventures.

About the Theme

Tim's Big Adventure illustrates the theme you can use your
imagination. Imagination can turn a bath into a deep-sea diving
adventure or cure a case of the blues on a rainy
day. After you read and discuss this
story, challenge your child to use
his or her imagination.

Reading the Story

Read *Tim's Big Adventure* with your child. Talk about what is happening in the pictures. Ask your child questions such as the following to assure comprehension of the story.

1. Why did the dolls have to stay inside? (Because it was raining.)
2. Who wanted to hear a story? (All the dolls except Tim.)
3. Was Babette really a prisoner in a castle? (No, just in Tim's imagination.)
4. Can Tallyho really fly? (No, just in Tim's imagination.)
5. How did the dragon stop the wizard? (By breathing fire and bursting his balloon.)

Reading Between the Lines

Ask your child to tell you how Tim felt when he learned that he couldn't go outside. How did he feel at the end of the story? What changed Tim's feelings? Point out that you can change a bad time into a good time just by using a little imagination. Ask your child which would be more fun—waiting to climb into the dentist's chair or waiting to board a moon rocket? One can be turned into the other with a little imagination!

Your Child and Imagining

Ask your child if he or she has ever imagined anything. Chances are the answer will be yes. Ask him or her to describe what it was like to use imagination. Expect examples such as ''Sometimes I pretend my doll is a real baby,'' ''I imagined the couch was a horse,'' or ''Sometimes I pretend that the dining room table is a fort.'' Explain that pretending is the same as using imagination.

Discuss the ways in which other people use their imaginations. Writers, for example, often make up stories in their imaginations before writing them down. Artists sometimes work from pictures in their imaginations.

Grow-and-Learn Activities

Little Green Men Ask your child to pretend that scientists have discovered a new planet called Blurp. They know there are people who live on Blurp, but they don't know what they look like. Ask your child to imagine a Blurpian family and then draw a picture of them. How many noses do they have? How many ears? What color are they? By the way, they are friendly!

What Do You See? Play a game of What Do You See with your child. Select an ordinary object and take turns telling what it *might* be. A footstool, for example, might be a horse, a cow that a cowboy could rope, a fort, a rock to hide behind, a doll's bed, or a table for a picnic. This game is limited only by your imaginations!

The Gwargs Are Coming! Ask your child to pretend that a new animal has been discovered. It has been named the Gwarg. Unfortunately, when someone tries to take a picture of a Gwarg, the camera breaks—Gwargs are very ugly. Have your child imagine what a Gwarg must look like and then make one out of modeling clay or play dough.

Grow-and-Learn Library

Another form of using your imagination is developed in Volume 13, *The Play in the Attic*, in which the characters use their imaginations to make the best of things.